W9-CDO-504

DISCARD

MACHINES

Go to Work in the City

WILLIAM LOW

HENRY HOLT AND COMPANY · NEW YORK

Vrooooom!

Here comes the garbage truck, making its run!

When the truck makes its last pickup,
are the garbage collectors done for the day?

No, they must go to the landfill
to empty the trash.

PSSSSSHHHHH!

In the train yard the engineer
checks the brakes.
The train is ready to go.

PSSSSSHHHHH!

In the train yard the engineer
checks the brakes.
The train is ready to go.

CRACK! CRACK!

A walkie-talkie crackles inside
a giant vacuum truck.
The driver answers the call.

No, flags mean CAUTION.
Workers are busy laying
new track.

Uh-oh! Yellow flags ahead.
The train slows down.
Is something wrong on the tracks?

A water pipe is broken in the tunnel below.
Will the vacuum truck fix the pipe?

BEEP! BEEP! HONK! HONK!

Cars and trucks stop when the traffic lights are not working.

A police officer moves
the traffic along.
Will the officer fix
the broken light?

No, when the bucket truck arrives, the signal crew will fix the traffic light.

RAT-TAT-TAT-TAT-TAT!

A tower crane lifts
the giant beams while
iron workers are busy below.

The building frame has grown as tall as the crane.
Can the crane operator still work?

No, construction must stop until the crane gets taller. New tower sections are lifted into place.

BEEP! BEEP! BEEP!

A baggage carrier rushes through
the busy airport lot.

The passengers are seated
with their bags on board.
Is the airplane ready to go?

No, the plane must be towed first.
The workers will signal when the
runway is clear.

"All systems go!"
The signalman watches as the plane
reaches for the sky!

Everyone in the plane sees
a beautiful sight.

Nighttime falls in the city below.
Tired workers return to their homes.

It's been a busy day for the city machines,
and tomorrow they will go to work again.

They see a river of sunshine,
a necklace of light.

Warning light

Baggage Carts

Back hitch

Baggage Carrier
Baggage carriers bring suitcases, boxes, and mail to planes. Extra cars can be added to move more luggage. Airport workers must wear ear protection because the jet engines are very loud.

Front hitch

Telescopic arm

Vacuum hose

Holding tank

Freshwater container

Extra hose section

Pump

Tool compartments

Freshwater hose

Vacuum Truck
Vacuum trucks suck garbage and water from clogged drains. The dirty water is held in a holding tank for safe disposal.

Bucket

Bucket controls

Rotating head

Rudder

Stabilizers

Bucket Truck
Bucket trucks lift workers up to repair traffic lights. They are also used to maintain telephone, cable, and electrical lines. The bucket can rotate for hard-to-reach places.

Hydraulic lifts

Emergency lights

Tool compartments

Stabilizers

Street Sweeper
Street sweepers keep the streets clean and free from garbage. Water is sprayed just before the street is swept to help control the dust.

Garbage container

Mirrors

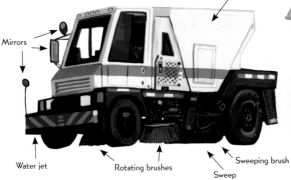

Water jet

Rotating brushes

Sweep

Sweeping brush

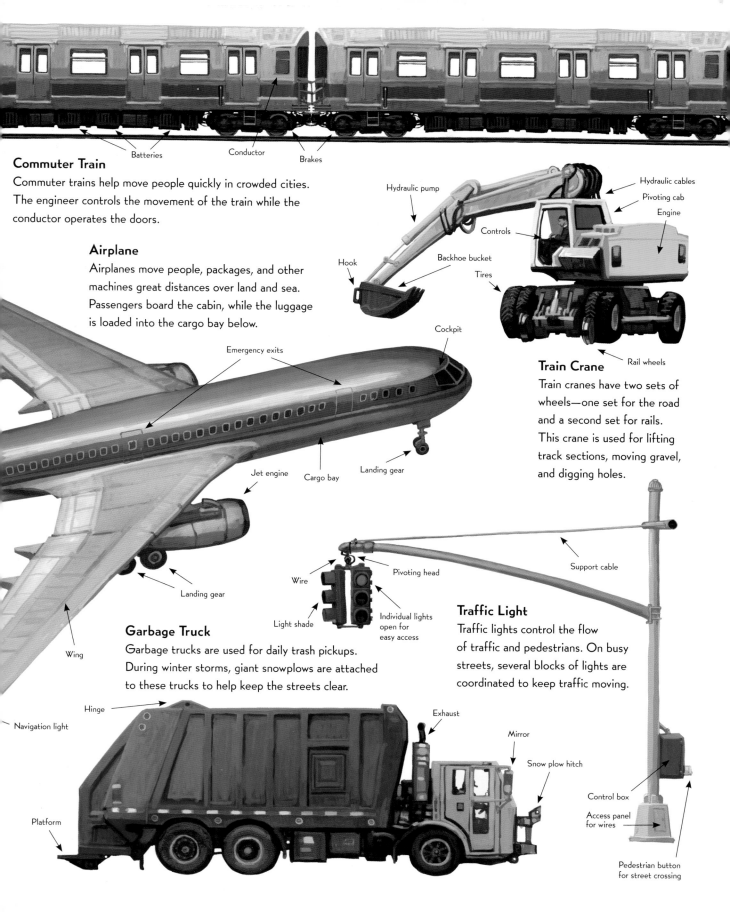

Batteries Conductor Brakes

Commuter Train

Commuter trains help move people quickly in crowded cities.
The engineer controls the movement of the train while the
conductor operates the doors.

Airplane

Airplanes move people, packages, and other
machines great distances over land and sea.
Passengers board the cabin, while the luggage
is loaded into the cargo bay below.

Hydraulic pump

Hydraulic cables

Pivoting cab

Engine

Controls

Hook Backhoe bucket

Tires

Cockpit

Emergency exits

Rail wheels

Train Crane

Train cranes have two sets of
wheels—one set for the road
and a second set for rails.
This crane is used for lifting
track sections, moving gravel,
and digging holes.

Jet engine Cargo bay Landing gear

Support cable

Wire Pivoting head

Light shade Individual lights
open for
easy access

Traffic Light

Traffic lights control the flow
of traffic and pedestrians. On busy
streets, several blocks of lights are
coordinated to keep traffic moving.

Landing gear

Garbage Truck

Garbage trucks are used for daily trash pickups.
During winter storms, giant snowplows are attached
to these trucks to help keep the streets clear.

Wing

Hinge

Navigation light

Exhaust

Mirror

Snow plow hitch

Control box

Access panel
for wires

Platform

Pedestrian button
for street crossing

Tower Crane

Tower cranes are short at the beginning of construction and grow as floors are added. This crane uses hydraulic jacks to lift itself and install a new tower section.

Cables to raise or lower boom

Counterweights to balance crane

Hoist for tower sections

New section

Telescopic mast

Axle for pivoting cab

Operator's cab

Boom

Mast

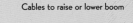

To Thomas, Claire, Allison, Peter, Jack, Aidan, Rhys, and Leah

Henry Holt and Company, LLC
Publishers since 1866
175 Fifth Avenue
New York, New York 10010
mackids.com

Library of Congress Cataloging-in-Publication Data
Low, William.
Machines go to work in the city / William Low. — 1st ed.
p.   cm.
ISBN 978-0-8050-9050-5 (hc)
1. Machinery—Juvenile literature. 2. Cities and towns—Juvenile literature.
3. Lift-the-flap books—Specimens. I. Title.
TJ147.L694 2012   621.8—dc23   2011029045

First Edition—2012 / Designed by Patrick Collins
Printed in China by South China Printing Co. Ltd.,
Dongguan City, Guangdong Province

10 9 8 7 6 5 4 3 2 1